TO STAY ALIVE

Books by Denise Levertov

Poetry

The Double Image

Here and Now

Overland to the Islands

With Eyes at the Back of Our Heads

The Jacob's Ladder

O Taste and See

The Sorrow Dance

Relearning the Alphabet

To Stay Alive

Translations

Guillevic/Selected Poems

Denise Levertov

To
Stay
Alive

A New Directions Book

ACKNOWLEDGMENTS

Some of these poems first appeared in the following publications:
Brown Bag, Hanging Loose, The Movement Towards a New America,
Mitchell Goodman, Ed., Alfred A. Knopf, 1970, *New Directions 23,*
Poetry, Rogue River Review and *Up From Under.* The "Olga Poems"
first appeared in *Poetry.* The quotation from Louis MacNeice in the
"Olga Poems" is from his *Solstices,* © 1961 by Louis MacNeice. Re-
printed by courtesy of Oxford University Press, Inc. The quotation
from Rainer Maria Rilke in "Life at War" is from *Letters of Rainer
Maria Rilke,* Volume Two, 1910–1926. Translated by Jane Bannard
Greene and M. D. Herter Norton. Copyright 1947, 1948 by W. W.
Norton & Company, Inc., New York, N.Y. Reprinted by permission
from the publisher. The quotation from José Yglesias in "Staying
Alive" is from his *In the Fist of the Revolution,* copyright © 1968
by José Yglesias. Reprinted by permission from Pantheon Books, a
Division of Random House, Inc. The quotation from Vladimir Maya-
kovsky in "Staying Alive" is from his *How Are Verses Made?* (Gross-
man Publishers, New York), copyright © 1970 by G. M. Hyde.
Reprinted by permission from Jonathan Cape, Ltd.

First published clothbound and as ND Paperbook 325 in 1971
Published simultaneously in Canada by McClelland & Stewart, Ltd.

Manufactured in the United States of America

New Directions Books are published for James Laughlin
by New Directions Publishing Corporation,
333 Sixth Avenue, New York 10014

Contents

As one goes on living and working, themes recur, transposed into another key perhaps. Single poems that seemed isolated perceptions when one wrote them prove to have struck the first note of a scale or a melody. I have heard professors of literature snicker with embarrassment because a poet quoted himself: they thought it immodest, narcissistic. Their attitude, a common one, reveals a failure to understand that though *the artist as craftsman* is engaged in making discrete and autonomous works—each of which, like a chair or a table, will have, as Ezra Pound said, the requisite number of legs and not wobble—yet at the same time, more unconsciously, as these attempts accumulate over the years, *the artist as explorer in language of the experiences of his or her life* is, willy-nilly, weaving a fabric, building a whole in which each discrete work is a part that functions in some way in relation to all the others. It happens at times that the poet becomes aware of the relationships that exist between poem and poem; is conscious, after the act, of one poem, one line or stanza, having been the precursor of another. It may be years later; and then, to get the design clear—'for himself and *thereby* for others,' Ibsen put it—he must in honesty pick up that thread, bring the cross reference into its rightful place in the inscape, the Gestalt of his life (his work)/his work (his life).

In *Relearning the Alphabet* I published some sections of a poem then called, as a working title, 'From a Notebook,' which I was aware was 'unfinished,' open-ended. In pursuing it further I came to realize that the long poem 'An Interim,' published in a different section of the same volume, was really a prelude or introduction to the Notebook poem. And Mitch Goodman and Hayden Carruth, on reading new parts of the Notebook, showed me that other, earlier poems—such as those I had written about my sister Olga after her death in 1964, and included in *The Sorrow Dance* —had a relation to it that seemed to demand their reissue in

vii

juxtaposition. It was Hayden who, years ago, pointed out to me how, in writing about my childhood in England, my diction became English—and this fact becomes itself one of the themes of the Notebook poem; for the sense my individual history gives me of being straddled between *places* extends to the more universal sense any writer my age— rooted in a cultural past barely shared by younger readers, yet committed to a solidarity of hope and struggle with the revolutionary young—must have of being almost unbearably, painfully, straddled across *time*.

In the pendant to 'Olga Poems'—'A Note to Olga, 1966,' two years after her death—occurs the first mention in my work of one of those public occasions, demonstrations, that have become for many of us such familiar parts of our lives. Later, not as a deliberate repetition but because the events were of importance to me, other such occasions were spoken of in other poems. The sense of community, of fellowship, experienced in the People's Park in Berkeley in 1969, deepened and intensified under the vicious police attack that, for middle-class whites especially, was so instructive. The personal response that moves from the identification of my lost sister, as a worker for human rights, with the pacifists 'going limp' as they are dragged to the paddywagon in Times Square in 1966, to the understanding by 1970 that 'there comes a time when only anger/is love,' is one shared by many of us who have come bit by bit to the knowledge that opposition to war, whose foul air we have breathed so long that by now we are almost choked forever by it, cannot be separated from opposition to the whole system of insane greed, of racism and imperialism, of which war is only the inevitable expression. In 'Prologue: An Interim' some of my heroes—that is, those who stand for integrity, honesty, love of life—are draft resisters who go to jail in testimony of their refusal to take part in carnage. In the same poem I invoked the self-immolators—Vietnamese and American—not as models but as flares to keep us moving in the dark. I spoke with love—a love I still feel—of those who 'disdain to kill.' But later I found that Gandhi himself had said it was better to 'cultivate the art of killing and being killed rather than in a cowardly manner to flee from danger.' In the later sections of the Notebook the sense of who the guardians of life, of integrity, are, is extended to include not only those who 'disdain to kill' but all who struggle, violently if need be, to pull down this obscene system before it destroys all life on earth.

The justification, then, of including in a new volume poems which are available in other collections, is esthetic—it assembles separated parts of a whole. And I am given courage to do so by the hope of that whole being seen as having some value not as mere 'confesssional' autobiography, but as a document of some historical value, a record of one person's inner/outer experience in America during the '60's and the beginning of the '70's, an experience which is shared by so many and transcends the peculiar details of each life, though it can only be expressed in and through such details.

DENISE LEVERTOV

PRELUDES

(Olga Levertoff, 1914–1964)

i

By the gas-fire, kneeling
to undress,
scorching luxuriously, raking
her nails over olive sides, the red
waistband ring—

(And the little sister
beady-eyed in the bed—
or drowsy, was I? My head
a camera—)

Sixteen. Her breasts
round, round, and
dark-nippled—

who now these two months long
is bones and tatters of flesh in earth.

ii

The high pitch of
nagging insistence, lines
creased into raised brows—

Ridden, ridden—
the skin around the nails
nibbled sore—

You wanted
to shout the world to its senses,
did you?—to browbeat

the poor into joy's
socialist republic—
What rage

and human shame swept you
when you were nine and saw
the Ley Street houses,

grasping their meaning as *slum*.
Where I, reaching that age,
teased you, admiring

architectural probity, circa
eighteen-fifty, and noted
pride in the whitened doorsteps.

Black one, black one,
there was a white
candle in your heart.

iii

i

Everything flows
                she muttered into my childhood,
pacing the trampled grass where human puppets
rehearsed fates that summer,
stung into alien semblances by the lash of her will—

everything flows—
I looked up from my Littlest Bear's cane armchair
and knew the words came from a book
and felt them alien to me

but linked to words we loved
                    from the hymnbook—*Time*
like an ever-rolling stream / bears all its sons away—

                    ii

Now as if smoke or sweetness were blown my way
I inhale a sense of her livingness in that instant,
feeling, dreaming, hoping, knowing boredom and zest like anyone
                                    else—
a young girl in the garden, the same alchemical square
I grew in, we thought sometimes
too small for our grand destinies—
                    But dread
was in her, a bloodbeat, it was against the rolling dark
oncoming river she raised bulwarks, setting herself
to sift cinders after early Mass all of one winter,

labelling her desk's normal disorder, basing
her verses on Keble's *Christian Year*, picking
those endless arguments, pressing on

to manipulate lives to disaster . . . To change,
to change the course of the river! What rage for order
disordered her pilgrimage—so that for years at a time

she would hide among strangers, waiting
to rearrange all mysteries in a new light.

iii

Black one, incubus—
      she appeared
riding anguish as Tartars ride mares

over the stubble of bad years.

In one of the years
      when I didn't know if she were dead or alive
I saw her in dream

haggard and rouged
            lit by the flare
from an eel- or cockle-stand on a slum street—

was it a dream? I had lost

all sense, almost, of
      who she was, what—inside of her skin,
under her black hair
                  dyed blonde—

it might feel like to be, in the wax and wane of the moon,
in the life I feel as unfolding, not flowing, the pilgrim years—

iv

On your hospital bed you lay
in love, the hatreds
that had followed you, a
comet's tail, burned out

as your disasters bred of love
burned out,
while pain and drugs
quarreled like sisters in you—

lay afloat on a sea
of love and pain—how you always
loved that cadence, 'Underneath
are the everlasting arms'—

all history
burned out, down
to the sick bone, save for

that kind candle.

v

i

In a garden grene whenas I lay—

you set the words to a tune so plaintive
it plucks its way through my life as through a wood.

As through a wood, shadow and light between birches,
gliding a moment in open glades, hidden by thickets of holly

your life winds in me.   In Valentines
a root protrudes from the greensward several yards from its tree

we might raise like a trapdoor's handle, you said,
and descend long steps to another country

where we would live without father or mother
and without longing for the upper world. *The birds
sang sweet,* O song, *in the midst of the daye,*

and we entered silent mid-Essex churches on hot afternoons
and communed with the effigies of knights and their ladies

and their slender dogs asleep at their feet,
the stone so cold—   *In youth*

is pleasure, in youth is pleasure.

ii

Under autumn clouds, under white
wideness of winter skies you went walking
the year you were most alone

returning to the old roads, seeing again
the signposts pointing to Theydon Garnon
or Stapleford Abbots or Greensted,

crossing the ploughlands (whose color I named *murple,*
a shade between brown and mauve that we loved
when I was a child and you

not much more than a child) finding new lanes
near White Roding or Abbess Roding; or lost in Romford's
new streets where there were footpaths then—

frowning as you ground out your thoughts, breathing deep
of the damp still air, taking
the frost into your mind unflinching.

8

How cold it was in your thin coat, your down-at-heel shoes—
tearless Niobe, your children were lost to you
and the stage lights had gone out, even the empty theater

was locked to you, cavern of transformation where all
had almost been possible.
                    How many books
you read in your silent lodgings that winter,
how the plovers transpierced your solitude out of doors with their
                                        strange cries
I had flung open my arms to in longing, once, by your side
stumbling over the furrows—

Oh, in your torn stockings, with unwaved hair,
you were trudging after your anguish
over the bare fields, soberly, soberly.

vi

Your eyes were the brown gold of pebbles under water.
I never crossed the bridge over the Roding, dividing
the open field of the present from the mysteries,
the wraiths and shifts of time-sense Wanstead Park held suspended,
without remembering your eyes. Even when we were estranged
and my own eyes smarted in pain and anger at the thought of you.
And by other streams in other countries; anywhere where the light
reaches down through shallows to gold gravel. Olga's
brown eyes. One rainy summer, down in the New Forest,
when we could hardly breathe for ennui and the low sky,
you turned savagely to the piano and sightread
straight through all the Beethoven sonatas, day after day—
weeks, it seemed to me. I would turn the pages some of the time,
go out to ride my bike, return—you were enduring in the

falls and rapids of the music, the arpeggios rang out, the rectory
trembled, our parents seemed effaced.
I think of your eyes in that photo, six years before I was born,
the fear in them. What did you do with your fear,
later? Through the years of humiliation,
of paranoia and blackmail and near-starvation, losing
the love of those you loved, one after another,
parents, lovers, children, idolized friends, what kept
compassion's candle alight in you, that lit you
clear into another chapter (but the same book) 'a clearing
in the selva oscura,
a house whose door
swings open, a hand beckons
in welcome'?
                    I cross
so many brooks in the world, there is so much light
dancing on so many stones, so many questions my eyes
smart to ask of your eyes, gold brown eyes,
the lashes short but the lids
arched as if carved out of olivewood, eyes with some vision
of festive goodness in back of their hard, or veiled, or shining,
unknowable gaze. . .

May–August, 1964

A Note to Olga (1966)

i

Of lead and emerald
the reliquary
that knocks my breastbone,

slung round my neck
on a rough invisible rope
that rubs the knob of my spine.

Though I forget you
a red coal from your fire
burns in that box.

ii

On the Times Square sidewalk
we shuffle along, cardboard signs
—Stop the War—
slung round our necks.

The cops
hurry about,
shoulder to shoulder,
comic.

Your high soprano
sings out from just
in back of me—

We shall—I turn,
you're, I very well know,
not there,

and your voice, they say,
grew hoarse
from shouting at crowds. . .

yet *overcome*
sounds then hoarsely
from somewhere in front,

the paddywagon
gapes. —It seems
you that is lifted

limp and ardent
off the dark snow
and shoved in, and driven away.

Life at War

The disasters numb within us
caught in the chest, rolling
in the brain like pebbles. The feeling
resembles lumps of raw dough

weighing down a child's stomach on baking day.
Or Rilke said it, 'My heart. . .
Could I say of it, it overflows
with bitterness . . . but no, as though

its contents were simply balled into
formless lumps, thus
do I carry it about.'
The same war

continues.
We have breathed the grits of it in, all our lives,
our lungs are pocked with it,
the mucous membrane of our dreams
coated with it, the imagination
filmed over with the gray filth of it:

the knowledge that humankind,

delicate Man, whose flesh
responds to a caress, whose eyes
are flowers that perceive the stars,

whose music excels the music of birds,
whose laughter matches the laughter of dogs,
whose understanding manifests designs
fairer than the spider's most intricate web,

still turns without surprise, with mere regret
to the scheduled breaking open of breasts whose milk
runs out over the entrails of still-alive babies,
transformation of witnessing eyes to pulp-fragments,
implosion of skinned penises into carcass-gulleys.

We are the humans, men who can make;
whose language imagines *mercy,
lovingkindness;* we have believed one another
mirrored forms of a God we felt as good—

who do these acts, who convince ourselves
it is necessary; these acts are done
to our own flesh; burned human flesh
is smelling in Vietnam as I write.

Yes, this is the knowledge that jostles for space
in our bodies along with all we
go on knowing of joy, of love;

our nerve filaments twitch with its presence
day and night,
nothing we say has not the husky phlegm of it in the saying,
nothing we do has the quickness, the sureness,
the deep intelligence living at peace would have.

What Were They Like?

1) Did the people of Vietnam
   use lanterns of stone?
2) Did they hold ceremonies
   to reverence the opening of buds?
3) Were they inclined to quiet laughter?
4) Did they use bone and ivory,
   jade and silver, for ornament?
5) Had they an epic poem?
6) Did they distinguish between speech and singing?

1) Sir, their light hearts turned to stone.
   It is not remembered whether in gardens
   stone lanterns illumined pleasant ways.
2) Perhaps they gathered once to delight in blossom,
   but after the children were killed
   there were no more buds.
3) Sir, laughter is bitter to the burned mouth.
4) A dream ago, perhaps. Ornament is for joy.
   All the bones were charred.
5) It is not remembered. Remember,
   most were peasants; their life
   was in rice and bamboo.
   When peaceful clouds were reflected in the paddies
   and the water buffalo stepped surely along terraces,
   maybe fathers told their sons old tales.
   When bombs smashed those mirrors
   there was time only to scream.
6) There is no echo yet
   of their speech which was like a song.
   It was reported their singing resembled
   the flight of moths in moonlight.
   Who can say? It is silent now.

15

Because in Vietnam the vision of a Burning Babe
is multiplied, multiplied,
                        the flesh on fire
not Christ's, as Southwell saw it, prefiguring
the Passion upon the Eve of Christmas,

but wholly human and repeated, repeated,
infant after infant, their names forgotten,
their sex unknown in the ashes,
set alight, flaming but not vanishing,
not vanishing as his vision but lingering,

cinders upon the earth or living on
moaning and stinking in hospitals three abed;

because of this my strong sight,
my clear caressive sight, my poet's sight I was given
that it might stir me to song,
is blurred.
                There is a cataract filming over
my inner eyes. Or else a monstrous insect
has entered my head, and looks out
from my sockets with multiple vision,

seeing not the unique Holy Infant
burning sublimely, an imagination of redemption,
furnace in which souls are wrought into new life,
but, as off a beltline, more, more senseless figures aflame.

And this insect (who is not there—
it is my own eyes do my seeing, the insect
is not there, what I see is there)
will not permit me to look elsewhere,

or if I look, to see except dulled and unfocused
the delicate, firm, whole flesh of the still unburned.

Tenebrae

(Fall of 1967)

Heavy, heavy, heavy, hand and heart.
We are at war,
bitterly, bitterly at war.

And the buying and selling
buzzes at our heads, a swarm
of busy flies, a kind of innocence.

Gowns of gold sequins are fitted,
sharp-glinting. What harsh rustlings
of silver moiré there are,
to remind me of shrapnel splinters.

And weddings are held in full solemnity
not of desire but of etiquette,
the nuptial pomp of starched lace;
a grim innocence.

And picnic parties return from the beaches
burning with stored sun in the dusk;
children promised a TV show when they get home
fall asleep in the backs of a million station wagons,
sand in their hair, the sound of waves
quietly persistent at their ears.
They are not listening.

Their parents at night
dream and forget their dreams.
They wake in the dark
and make plans. Their sequin plans
glitter into tomorrow.
They buy, they sell.

17

They fill freezers with food.
Neon signs flash their intentions
into the years ahead.

And at their ears the sound
of the war. They are
not listening, not listening.

Enquiry

You who go out on schedule
to kill, do you know
there are eyes that watch you,
eyes whose lids you burned off,
that see you eat your steak
and buy your girlflesh
and sell your PX goods
and sleep?
She is not old,
she whose eyes
know you.
She will outlast you.
She saw
her five young children
writhe and die;
in that hour
she began to watch you,
she whose eyes are open forever.

STAYING ALIVE

i

While the war drags on, always worse,
the soul dwindles sometimes to an ant
rapid upon a cracked surface;

lightly, grimly, incessantly
it skims the unfathomed clefts where despair
seethes hot and black.

ii

Children in the laundromat
waiting while their mothers fold sheets.
A five-year-old boy addresses
a four-year-old girl. 'When I say,
Do you want some gum? say *yes.*'
'Yes . . .' 'Wait!—Now:
Do you want some gum?'
'Yes!' 'Well yes means no,
so you can't have any.'
He chews. He pops a big, delicate bubble at her.

O language, virtue
of man, touchstone
worn down by what
gross friction . . .

                    And,
' "It became necessary
to destroy the town to save it,"
a United States major said today.
He was talking about the decision
by allied commanders to bomb and shell the town
regardless of civilian casualties,
to rout the Vietcong.'

21

O language, mother of thought,
are you rejecting us as we reject you?

Language, coral island
accrued from human comprehensions,
human dreams,

you are eroded as war erodes us.

iii

To repossess our souls we fly
to the sea. To be reminded
of its immensity, and the immense sky
in which clouds move at leisure,
transforming their lives ceaselessly,
sternly, playfully.

*Today is the 65th day since de Courcy Squire, war-resister,
began her fast in jail. She is 18.*

And the sun
is warm bread, good to us, honest.
And the sand gives itself to our feet
or to our outstretched bodies,
hospitable, accommodating, its shells
unendingly at hand for our wonder.

*. . . arrested with 86 others Dec. 7. Her crime:
sitting down in front of a police wagon
momentarily preventing her friends from being
hauled to prison. Municipal Judge Heitzler
handed out 30-day suspended sentences to several others
accused of the same offense, but condemned
Miss Squire to 8 months in jail and fined her
$650. She had said in court 'I don't think there should be
roles like judge and defendant.'*

Peace as grandeur. Energy
serene and noble. The waves
break on the packed sand,

butterflies take the cream o' the foam,
from time to time a palmtree lets fall
another dry branch, calmly.
                              The restlessness
of the sound of waves
transforms itself in its persistence
to that deep rest.
                    At fourteen
after measles my mother took me
to stay by the sea. In the austere presence

of Beachy Head we sat long hours
close to the tideline. She read aloud
from George Eliot, while I half-dozed
and played with pebbles. Or I read
to myself Richard Jefferies'
The Story of My Heart, which begins

in such majesty.
                  I was mean and grouchy
much of the time, but she forgave me,

and years later remembered
only the peace of that time.

The quiet there is
in listening.
              Peace could be

that grandeur, that dwelling
in majestic presence, attuned
to the great pulse.

The cocks crow all night
far and near. Hoarse with expectation.
And by day stumble red-eyed in the dust
where the heat flickers its lizard tongue.

In my dream the city
was half Berlin, half Chicago—
midwest German, Cincinnati perhaps,
where de Courcy Squire is.
There were many of us
jailed there, in moated fortresses—
five of them, with monosyllabic
guttural names. But by day
they led us through the streets,
dressed in our prisoners' robes—
smocks of brown holland—
and the people watched us pass
and waved to us, and gave us
serious smiles of hope.

Between us and the beach
a hundred yards of trees, bushes, buildings,
cut the breeze. But at the *verge*
of the salt flood, always
a steady wind, prevailing.

While we await your trial,
(and this is no dream) we are

free to come and go. To rise
from sleep and love and dreams about
ambiguous circumstance, and from
waking in darkness to cockcrow, and moving
deliberately (by keeping still) back into
morning sleep; to rise and float

24

into the blue day, the elaborate rustlings
of the palmtrees way overhead; to hover
with black butterflies at the lemon-blossom.
The sea awaits us; there are sweet oranges
on our plates; the city grayness has been
washed off our skins, we take pleasure
in each other's warmth of rosy brown.

vi

'Puerto Rico, Feb. 23, 1968.

. . . Some people, friends sincerely
concerned for us but who don't seem to understand what
it's really all about, apparently feel sorry for us because
Mitch has been indicted. One letter this morning said,
shyly and abruptly, after talking about quite unrelated mat-
ters, "My heart aches for you." Those people don't understand that however boring the trial will be in some ways,
and however much of a distraction, as it certainly is, from
the things one's nature would sooner be engaged with, yet
it's quite largely a kind of pleasure too, a relief, a satisfac-
tion of the need to confront the war-makers and, in the
process, do something to wake up the bystanders.
. . . Mitch and the others have a great deal of support,
people who think of them as spokesmen; they have good
lawyers, and have had and will have a lot of publicity of the
kind one hopes will be useful—I don't mean useful for their
case, saving them from going to jail, I mean useful towards
clarifying the issues, stopping the draft, helping to end the
war.'

But something like a cramp
of fury begins to form

(in the blue day, in the sweetness
of life we float in, allowed
this interim before the trial)
a cramp of fury at the mild,
saddened people whose hearts ache
not for the crimes of war,
the unspeakable—of which, then,
I won't speak—
and not for de Courcy Squire's
solitary passion
                    but for us.

Denied visitors, even her parents;
confined to a locked cell without running water
or a toilet.
                    On January 29th, the 53rd day of her fast,
Miss Squire was removed to a hospital.
All the doctors would do was inform her that
the fast may cause her permanent brain injury.

'The sympathy of mild good folk,
a kind of latex from their leaves;
our inconvenience draws it out.

The white of egg without the yolk,
it soothes their conscience and relieves
the irritations of their doubt.'

. . . You see how it is—I am angry that they feel no outrage.
Their feeling flows in the wrong directions and at the wrong
intensity. And all I can bring forth out of my anger is a
few flippant rhymes. What I want to tell you—no, not you,
you understand it; what I want them to grasp is that though
I understand that Mitch may have to go to jail and that it
will be a hard time for him and for me, yet, because it's for

doing what we know we must do, that hardship is imagi-
nable, encompassable, and a small thing in the face of the
slaughter in Vietnam and the other slaughter that will come.
And there is no certainty he will go to jail.'

And the great savage saints of outrage—
who have no lawyers,
who have no interim
in which to come and go,
for whom there is no world left—
their bodies rush upon the air in flames,
sparks fly, fragments of charred rag
spin in the whirlwind, a vacuum
where there used to be this monk or that,
Norman Morrison, Alice Hertz.

Maybe they are crazy. I know I could never
bring myself to injure my own flesh, deliberately.
And there are other models of behavior
to aspire to—A. J. Muste did not burn himself
but worked through a long life to make from outrage
islands of compassion others could build on.
Dennis Riordon, Bob Gilliam, how many others,
are alive and free in the jails. Their word is good,
language draws breath again in their *yes* and *no*,
true testimony of love and resistance.

But we need
the few who could bear no more,
who would try anything,
who would take the chance
that their deaths among the uncountable
masses of dead might be real to those who
don't dare imagine death.
Might burn through the veil that blinds
those who do not imagine the burned bodies
of other people's children.

We need them.
Brands that flare to show us
the dark we are in,
to keep us moving in it.

vii

To expand again, to plunge
our dryness into the unwearying source—

but not to forget.
Not to forget but to remember better.

We float in the blue day
darkly. We rest behind half-closed louvers,
the hot afternoon clouds up,
the palms hold still.

'I have a medical problem that can be cured'—
Miss Squire said last week when she was removed
from the city workhouse to Cincinnati General Hospital,
'I have a medical problem that can be cured
only by freedom.'

Puerto Rico, February–March, 1968

i

Revolution or death. Revolution or death.
Wheels would sing it
                            but railroads are obsolete,
we are among the clouds, gliding, the roar
a toneless constant.
                    Which side are you on?
Revolution, of course. Death is Mayor Daley.
This revolution has no blueprints, and
                    ('What makes this night different
                    from all other nights?')
is the first that laughter and pleasure aren't shot down in.

Life that
            wants to live.
                                (Unlived life
                    of which one can die.)
                I want the world to go on
            unfolding. The brain
not gray except in death, the photo I saw
of prismatic radiance pulsing from live tissue.
                I see Dennis Riordon and de Courcy Squire,
                gentle David Worstell, intransigent Chuck Matthei
                blowing angel horns at the imagined corners.
            Jennie Orvino singing
            beatitudes in the cold wind
                            outside a Milwaukee courthouse.
I want their world—in which they already live,
they're not waiting for demolition and reconstruction.
                                'Begin here.'
Of course I choose
revolution.

ii

And yet, yes, there's the death
that's not the obscene sellout, the coprophiliac spasm
that smears the White House walls with its desensitized
                                                  thumbs.

      Death lovely,
      whispering,
      a drowsy numbness . . .
                    'tis not
      from envy of thy happy lot
                    lightwingéd dryad . . .

Even the longest river . . .

Revolution or death. Love
aches me.   *. . . river*
winds somewhere to the sea.

iii

Shining of Lorie's hair, swinging
        alive, color of new copper—

who has died and risen.
'What am I doing here? I had died—'
(The nurses are frightened. The doctor
refuses to tell what happened those four hours.)
whose body at twenty-three is at war
within itself
trying to die again,

whose 'psychic energy' pulls her ten ways:
sculpture   poetry   painting
psychology   photography   teaching
cookery   love   Chinese philosophy
physics

      If she can live I can live.

iv

Trying one corner after another
to flag down a cab
                        at last unthinking as one at last
                        seems to see me,
                                        I run into the traffic—
screech of brakes,
human scream, mine,
anger of drivers and shocked pedestrians
yelling at me!
                Is that how death is,
                that poor, that trivial? I'm
not even frightened, only ashamed,
the driver almost refusing me,
scolding me half the way to the airport, I
strenuous to convince him I'm not
a habitual public danger.
So close to death and thinking only
of being forgiven by strangers.

v

Gliding among clouds.   The will to live
pulses.   Radiant emanations
of living tissue, visible only
to some photo-eye we know
sees true because mind's dream-eye,
inward gage, confirms it.
                Confirmation,
a sacrament.

                Around the Fish
(it's reproduced here in the magazine the air-hostess gives me)
                rearranges itself as *Around the—*
                Nature of Death, is it? *How*
                to Live, What to Do?

after yet another return home,
first thing I see is a picture postcard
that stood on the windowledge all summer,
somehow not seen. An Assyrian relief. The wings
(as I look at the words I've written, 'gliding among clouds')
draw me to pick it up and examine it:
a sturdy muscular being it shows,
thick-bearded, heavy-sandalled;
wings made for crossing from world to world.
His hair is bound with a wreath;
in his left hand he grips
a thickstemmed plant bearing five blossoms.

Who sent him?

I turn the card over—ah! at once
I know the hand—Bill Rose's. This was his message to me,
six months ago, unanswered. Is now the newly dead—
less than three weeks—trying to speak to me
one last time?

How to live and the will to live,
what was recalled to me of those
rainbow pulsations some Russian scientist
discovered,
the choosing
always before me now that sings itself
quietly, *revolution or death*
cluster about some center
unknown, shifting but retaining—
snowflake forms in a kaleidescope—
a character that throughout all transformations
reveals them connatural.

And to that cluster

this winged genie from Nimrud
now adds himself,
last sign from a friend whose life
failed him in some way long before death:

32

a man my age
a man deeply dissatisfied
as he told me once.

       'It came on very suddenly; he
found out at the end of the summer that nothing could be
done for him, so to make the waiting easier, he decided to
go on teaching. But within a few weeks of that decision, he
was dead.'
      And someone else writes: 'Mr Rose was such a
lone figure; he lived alone; you mostly saw him alone; and
that's what's so hard to take: he died alone. I never knew
him except by sight.'

    Is there anything
    I write any more that is not
    elegy?
          Goldengrove
is unleaving all around me; I live
in goldengrove; all day
yesterday and today the air has been filled
with that hesitant downwardness;
the marigolds, the pumpkin, must be sought out
to be seen, the grass
is covered with that cloth, the roads'
margins illuminated.

vi

Learned—not for the first time—my 'roots in the
19th century' put me
          out of touch.

Born in the '20's, but a late child, my parents' memories
pivoting on their first meeting, Constantinople, 1910, and
returning into the '90's. Reading, I went straight from
Grimm and Andersen to the 19th-century novel. Until the

war—1939—there was a muffin-man who came by in foggy
winter dusks, tea-time, ringing his bell, his wares balanced
on his head according to the mysteries of his trade as if
Dickens were still alive—
The 'Ode to a Nightingale' was the first and only poem I
ever learned by heart. Thus, when I wrote, translating,
'*purged* of legend,' the reader's thought was of Stalin, while
my intention was something more graphic than the literal
'cured'—

and again when I said the sun approached
'to study the flower,' the reader—

> to whom I would give
> all that arms can hold, eyes
> encompass—

alas, thought of a tedious process,
grade-points, term-papers—while I had meant 'study—e.g.,

> I study your face intently
> > but its secret eludes me,'
> or, 'he took her hand and studied
> the strong fingers, the veins,
> the curious ring.'

Without a terrain in which, to which, I belong,
language itself is my one home, my Jerusalem,

yet time and the straddled ocean
undo me, maroon me,
(roadblocks, the lines down)—

> > I choose
> > > revolution but my words

often already don't reach forward

> > into it—
> > > (perhaps)

> Whom I would touch
> I may not,

34

whom I may
I would
but often do not.

My diction marks me
untrue to my time;
change it, I'd be
untrue to myself.
                    I study
a face intently.
Learning.
Beginning to learn.
And while
        I study,
                O, in that act
of passionate attention
A *drowsy numbness*
pains my sense.
                Too happy in thy happiness.
Love of living.   *That wants to live.*   *Unlived life.*
whisper
of goldengrove . . .

i

Last of October, light thinning
towards the cold. Deep shadow.

Yellow honey, the ridge, a grove 'thrown into relief,'
of tamaracks, lurid, glamorous
upon the breast of
moving darkness, clouds thick with
gunmetal blue.
It becomes
November without one's knowing it.
Broad rays from southwest-by-west
single out one by one
the fixed parts of earthscape.

And into the first snowstorm   (marooned)
the lines down
no phone
no lights
no heat
gastank for cooking about to give out
car stuck in the driveway.

       We find candles.
       We light up the woodstove which was all we
       used to have anyway, till a few weeks back.

ii

A fly I thought dead
on its back on the windowsill,
grayed, shrivelled,

slowly waves.
Yes, what would be its right arm
dreamily moves—out—in—out again
twice, three times.
It seems
flies dream in dying.

iii

Four p.m.—pleasure
in exercise
in air,
in sound of brook
under and out from
thin ice

pleasure
of chest and shoulders
pushing air that's
not cold enough to hurt.

Jumping
into snowbank—
no sound—

pleasure—

But to the eye
terror of a kind:

black-and-white photo world
not night yet
but at four p.m.
no light we know

hemlock and cedar a toneless black,
snowtufted trunks and boughs
black, sky white, birches
whiter, snow
infinitely whiter: all things
muted: deprived
of color, as if
color were utterance.
A terror
as of eclipse.
The whites graying.

iv

George told me, and then I read it in Beckett,
Proust had a bad memory,
                              the only kind worth having,
Beckett argues: there's no remembrance
                    and so no revelation,
    for those Admirable, terrifying, unimaginable Crichtons
    who don't disremember nothing, keep
    the whole works in mind.
No pain. No sharp stabs of recall. No revelation.

I stretch in luxury; knowledge of the superb badness
of my memory gives me a sense of having thick fur,
a tail, and buried somewhere
a sweet bone, rotten, enticing . . .

What pain! What sharp stabs of recall! What revelations!
The black taste of life, the music
angel tongues buzz when my paws nuzzle it
out into light!

v

Again to hold—'capture' they say—
moments and their processions in palm
of mind's hand.
    Have you ever,
in stream or sea,
    felt the silver of fish
pass through your hand-hold? not to stop it,
block it from going onward, but feel it
move in its wave-road?
    To make
   of song a chalice,
    of Time,
  a communion wine.

Part II

Can't go further.
If there's to be a
second part, it's not
a going beyond, I'm
still here.

To dig down,
to re-examine.

. . . .

What is the revolution I'm driven
to name, to live in? —that now roars,
a toneless constant, now
sings itself?

It's in the air: no air
to breathe without
scent of it,
pervasive:
odor of snow,
freshwater,
stink of dank
vegetation recomposing.

—Yet crisply
the moon's risen,
full, complete.
Secret uprising (last time I looked,
surely not long since,
dark was
as complete).
The snowfields have been
taken over

(glistening crust of ice upon snow
in driftwaves, curves of stilled
wind-caress, bare to the moon
in silence of adoration).

　　　　　If it were so for us!
　　　　　But that's the moon's world.

　　　　·　·　·　·　·　·　·

Robert reminds me *revolution*
implies the circular: an exchange
of position, the high
brought low, the low
ascending, a revolving,
an endless rolling of the wheel. The wrong word.
We use the wrong word. A new life
isn't the old life in reverse, negative of the same photo.
But it's the only
word we have . . .

　　　　·　·　·　·　·　·　·

Chuck Matthei
travels the country
　　　　　a harbinger.
(He's 20. His golden beard was pulled and clipped
　　　by a Wyoming sheriff, but no doubt has grown
　　　　　　　　　　　　　　　　　　again
　　　though he can't grow knocked-out teeth.
　　　He wears sneakers even in winter,
　　　　to avoid animal-hide; etc.)
And on his journeyings bears
my poem 'A Man'
to prisoners in the jails.
　　　　　Of Mitch I wrote it,

41

even before anyone heard
the voice he
brought to song.
But Chuck has found in it
a message for all who resist war,
disdain to kill,
try to equate
'human' with 'humane.'
(And if his intransigeance
brings us another despair
and we call it 'another form of aggression,'
don't we confess—
wishing he had a sense of humor—
our own extremity?)

'Living a life' the poem begins.
'—the beauty of deep lines
dug in your cheeks'
and ends,
'you pick out
your own song from the uproar,

line by line,
and at last throw back
your head and sing it.'
Next on the mimeograph follows:
'THERE IS ONLY AS MUCH PEACE AS THERE ARE
PEACEFUL PEOPLE'
(A. J. Muste)
Then Chuck has written:
This is your only life—live it well!

No one man can bring about a social change—
but each man's life is a whole and necessary part of his
society,
a necessary step in any change,
and a powerful example of the possibility of life
for others.

Let all of our words and our actions speak the possibility of
  peace and cooperation between men.
Too long have we used the excuse:
  'I believe in peace, but that other man does not—when
  he lays down his arms, then I will follow.'

  Which of us deserves to wait to be the last good man
  on earth; how long will we wait if all of us wait?

Let each man begin a one-man revolution of peace and
  mutual aid—so that there is at least that much peace . . .
  a beginning; . . .

A beginning.
Where shall we
begin?
Can't go
further.
             Time, says the old Canon,
in Denis Saurat's *Death and the Dreamer*,
             is not a sequence,
             as man's simplicity thinks, but radiates
out from a center
                   every direction,
                   all
                       dimensions
                              (pulsations, as from living cells,
radiant—

             .   .   .   .

May 14th, 1969—Berkeley
Went with some of my students to work in the People's
Park. There seemed to be plenty of digging and gardening
help so we decided, as Jeff had his truck available, to shovel
up the garbage that had been thrown into the west part of
the lot and take it out to the city dump.

O happiness
in the sun! Is it
that simple, then,
to live?
—crazy rhythm of
scooping up barehanded
(all the shovels already in use)
careless of filth and broken glass
—scooping up garbage together
poets and dreamers studying
joy together, clearing
refuse off the neglected, newly recognized,
humbly waiting ground, place, locus, of what could be our
New World even now, our revolution, one and one and
one and one together, black children swinging, green
guitars, that energy, that music, no one
telling anyone what to do,
everyone doing,

each leaf of
the new grass near us
a new testament . . .

Out to the dump:
acres of garbage glitter and stink in wild sunlight, gulls
float and scream in the brilliant sky,
polluted waters bob and dazzle, we laugh, our arms ache,
we work together
shoving and kicking and scraping to empty our truckload
over the bank
even though we know
the irony of adding to the Bay fill, the System has us there—
but we love each other and return to the Park.

Thursday, May 15th
At 6 a.m. the ominous zooming, war-sound, of helicopters
breaks into our sleep.

To the Park:
ringed with police.
Bulldozers have moved in.
Barely awake, the people—
those who had made for each other
a green place—
begin to gather at the corners.

Their tears fall on sidewalk cement.
The fence goes up, twice a man's height.
Everyone knows (yet no one yet
believes it) what all shall know
this day, and the days that follow:
now, the clubs, the gas,
bayonets, bullets. The War
comes home to us . . .

.   .   .   .

WHAT PEOPLE CAN DO

1. Be in the streets—they're ours!
2. Report any action you have witnessed or been involved in that should be broadcast to keep the people informed. Especially call to report the location of any large groups of people, so those people who have been separated may regroup . . .
3. The Free Church and Oxford Hall medical aid stations need medical supplies, especially:
   —gauze pads
   —adhesive tape
   —plastic squeeze bottles.
4. PLEASE do not go to the Free Church unless you have need to.
5. Photographers and filmmakers: Contact Park Media Committee.
6. Bail money will be collected at tables outside the COOP grocery stores:
   —Telegraph Ave. store: Monday
   —University Ave. store: Tuesday
   —Shattuck Ave. store: Wed. & Thurs.
7. BRING YOUR KITE AND FLY IT. Use nylon strings. Fly it when you are with a crowd. A helicopter cannot fly too near flying kites.
8. Be your brothers' and sisters' keeper.
9. Take care.

'change is now
change is now
things that seem to be solid are not'

The words came through, transistor
turned up loud. The music, the beat,
lost now, but
the words hang on.

Revolution: a crown of tree
              raises itself out of the heavy
              flood.
                    A branch lifts
                    under null skies' weight
              pushes against
              walls of air, flashing
              clefts in it.

The floodwaters
stir, mud
swirls to the surface.

              A hand, arm,
              lifts in the crawl—
              hands, arms, intricate
                    upflashing—
                              a sea full of swimmers!
                    their faces' quick steady
                    lift for air—
Maybe what seems
evanescent is solid.

Islands
step out of the waves on rock feet.

i   **At the Justice Department**
     November 15, 1969

Brown gas-fog, white
beneath the street lamps.
Cut off on three sides, all space filled
with our bodies.
    Bodies that stumble
in brown airlessness, whitened
in light, a mildew glare,
      that stumble
hand in hand, blinded, retching.
Wanting it, wanting
to be here, the body believing it's
dying in its nausea, my head
clear in its despair, a kind of joy,
knowing this is by no means death,
is trivial, an incident, a
fragile instant.   Wanting it, wanting
     with all my hunger this anguish,
      this knowing in the body
the grim odds we're
up against, wanting it real.
Up that bank where gas
curled in the ivy, dragging each other
up, strangers, brothers
and sisters.   Nothing
will do but
to taste the bitter
taste. No life
other, apart from.

ii   Gandhi's Gun (and Brecht's Vow)

Vessels of several
shapes and sizes—

bowls, pots,
a tall vase

and the guitar's
waiting body:

forms drawn
by a hand's
energy.

      'Never

         run away from the stormcenter.

        Cultivate

        cool courage, die without killing—'

Strong orange, deep
oil-pastel green

but at the center, strange
upstroke of black

stronger, deeper
than all.
         —'but if one has not

        that courage'—

(or singing, '*Keiner
oder Alle, Alles
oder Nichts!*')
            —'cultivate

    the art of killing and being killed

    rather than in a cowardly manner

                to flee from danger.'

Vessels, counterparts
of the human; primal
vessel of music

towards which like a rifle
that harsh stroke blackly
points upward

would fail, fall from their whirling
dance, without

the terror patiently
poised there,

ultimate focus.

iii   The Year One

Arn says it's
the Year one.

And I
know such violent

revolution has ached
my marrowbones, my

soul changing
its cells, my

cracked heart tolling
such songs of

unknown morning-star
ecstatic anguish, the clamor

of unquenched desire's
radiant decibels shattering

the patient wineglasses
set out by private history's ignorant

quiet hands,   —I keep
enduring such pangs of giving

birth or being
born,
        I dream

maybe he's right.

'Tell Denise to write about the devil.'

i

Tell Sam
it is (perhaps) the devil
made me so goddamned strong

that I have made myself
(almost)
numb,
almost unable
to feel in me
(for now)
the beautiful outreaching of desire.

And tell him
it is perhaps the devil
inserted these parenthetical
qualifications.

ii

It's the devil
swarms into 'emptiness'
not
    waiting
        until it slowly
        as a jar let stand
        at fountain's edge, fills,
        drop by drop,
but busily, as if not water
but flies buzzing were what
'emptiness' were to hold.

iii

Looking for the devil I walked
down Webster St. and across on
Cottage St. and down
Sumner to Maverick Square
and saw
3 dogs nosing the green plastic
    garbage bags on the sidewalk,
5 children screaming cheerfully together, sliding
                        upon a strip of gray ice,
1 simpleton (Webster St.'s own) who waved and called
                            'Hi!' to me,
4 elderly Italian peasant women (separately)
                    lugging home groceries
    in big shopping bags, their faces solemn
                    as at some ritual,
2 twelve-year-old girls in cheap maxicoats,
10 more or less silent teen-aged boys
                    in groups of 3 or 4 standing
    on several corners, collars up, seeming
                    to wait for something which
    was not about to happen,
2 middle-aged bookies, one wearing
    a seedy chesterfield—the same guys I saw
    one day at the Buffalo Meat Market ordering
    some big steaks, but today
    down on their luck—

and no doubt some other persons, but these
were all I noticed:
and in none of these
could I discern the devil
(under the sullen January sky) nor was the devil,
surely, the east wind
blowing garbage out of the bags after
the dogs succeeded in ripping them,
nor was the devil the ugly
dogshit innocently smeared on the pavement.

54

Was he then
my eyes that searched for him?
Or was he the inexorable
smog of tedium that we breathed,
I and all these, even
the children at play, even, quite possibly, the dogs?

Or was he
the toneless ignorance all that I saw
had of itself?

v   Today

Just feeling human
the way a cloud's a cloud
tinged with blue or
walking slow across the sky or
hastening,
but not a Thursday cloud
formed for the anxious glance of Thursday people,
simply a cloud, whose particles
may fall Tuesday, just as well,
on anyone's springy hair, on any
taciturn winter buds it chooses
and no one say no. Human,
free for the day from roles assigned,
each with its emblem
cluttering the right hand,
scroll of words in the left.
Human, a kind of element, a fire,
an air, today.
Floating up to you I enter, or you
enter me. Or imagine
a house without doors,
open to sun or snowdrifts.

vi   Casa Felice (I)

Getting back into
ordinary gentle morning, tide
        wavelessly dreaming in,
        silent gulls at ease on wheatsheaf sandbars—

Off the limb of
desperation
            I drop
            plumb into peace for a day—

it's
    not easy.
            But easier—
                    O blesséd
                    blue!
            —than fear and reason
            supposed of late.

vii   Casa Felice (II)

Richard, if you were here
would you too be peaceful?

*(I am angry
all of the time, not just sometimes,
you said. We must
smash the state.
Smash the state.)*

If you were here
for these two days at Casa
Felice, if you were here and listened
to the almost soundless tide
incoming,
            what would it say to you?

56

Would you feel new
coldness towards me
because this April morning, gentle light
on the unglittering sea and pale sands,
I am not angry and not tense?

viii   Revolutionary

When he said
'Your struggle is my struggle'
a curtain was pushed away.

A curtain was pushed away revealing
an open window
and beyond that

an open country.
For the first time I knew it was actual.
I was indoors still

but the air from fields
beyond me touched my face.

It was a country
of hilly fields, of many
shadows and rivers.

The thick heavy dark
curtain had hidden
a world from me;

curtain of sorrow, world
where far-off I see
people moving—

struggling to move, as I
towards my window
struggle, burdened but not

each alone. They move
out in that air together
where I too

will be moving,
not alone.

ix   'I Thirst'

Beyond the scaffolding set up for
TV cameras, a long way
from where I sit among 100,000 reddening
white faces,
            is a big wooden cross:

and strapped upon it, turning
his head from side to side in pain
in the 90-degree shadeless Washington midafternoon
May 9th, 1970,
            a young black man.

'We must *not* be angry, we must
L-O-O-O-V-E!' Judy Collins
bleats loud and long into the P.A. system,

but hardly anyone claps, and no one
shouts *Right On.*
            That silence cheers me.
Judy, understand:
there comes a time when only anger
is love.

i

Silver summer light of Trieste early evening

> (a silver almost gold
> almost grey).

Caffè,
little cup
black and sweet.

> The waiter
> tall and benevolent
> gives some change to a wanderer
> (not a beggar,
> he has a pack,
> is maybe 30 and
> no taller than a boy of 11).
> Almost weeping with weariness.
> Stands to gaze at a green plant.
> Droops.
> Sinks to the pavement.
> The waiter
gently sends him across the street
to a marble bench set in the church wall.

'Where is he from, that man?'
A shrug—'É Italiano . . .'

Maybe from Sicily. Later I pause
to watch him
curled like a tired child on the stone.

.

Caffè, another
sweet and black
little cup.

Cop-out, am I,
or merely,
        as the day fades

        (and Amerika
        far away
        tosses in fever)

on holiday?

ii

                And David said
                in England

                What's a cop-out? Is it
                the same as
                opting out?

                And I said
                Yes, but
                opting out sounds like
                cool choice

                and copping-out
                means fear and weakness

but he said
No,
we mean that too.

iii

Strange, a rusty freight train's passing
between the cafés and the sea
(a long train of cars
veiled in old Europe's dust—maybe
they've shuttled up and down the Adriatic
since before the War, and inland,
anywhere)

cutting between the sidewalk tables
                and the view
to no one's surprise but mine

and when they've gone by
the dim sea
has vanished,

vague silver
tarnished to blue;

points of amber
show where the suburbs
drift over down-grey hills.

iv

Summer dusk,
Triestino,
deep blue now.

The port, its commerce:
a few gold bars
broken upon the water.

A ship from Genoa
riding at anchor.
Port light, starboard.

The sky   the water
    warm   blue   blurred.

v

On the broad Riva
among young couples
taking the air with their babies

men still prowl as they used to,
laughably. Buona sera. Buona sera, Signorina.
                    (That spring of '48, the weeks
                    alone in Florence, waiting for Mitch.
                    And I used to talk to the Israeli terrorist,
                    if that's what he was, in the Pensione,
                    but the Signora told me to watch out for him,
                    a young bride should watch out.)
                                        Buona sera.
No sexual revolution here, no Women's Lib.
That's the third car to slow down.
        (The difference is, more cars,
        new ones too, I see.)
Buona sera, signorina. Each driver
leans out, affable.
                    Evidently
I must give up my
slow stroll.

(And in me the difference
is, I'm not scared,
I find them only foolish, they're
in my way.

But do they spend every evening
cruising?   No whores around,
too early maybe. Whom do they
hope for?)

I turn briskly along a one-way street.
In the hotel lobby, *terza classe,*
a young man, thickly handsome,
looks at me over the *Corriere della Sera*
and jumps up to follow me
but I get upstairs to my door and in and
shut it, just as his mechanical shadow
precedes him into the corridor.

'*Honestly!* I *ask* you!'
some English voice laughs in my head.

Buona notte.

vi

Back in Boston a month ago I wrote:

'At my unhappiest,
like the next guy, I want

oblivion

but even when
a couple of sleeping pills or
total immersion in an almost-boring fiction

          at last succeed in
shutting my eyes and
whatever torment ails me shuts off
and I get what I wanted

oblivion,

          I don't want it for long.
                    I don't know
how to be mute, or deaf, or blind,
for long, but
wake and plunge into next day
talking, even if I say *yesterday* when I mean *tomorrow*,
listening, even if what I'm hearing
has the *approaching* sound of terror,
seeing, even if the morning light
and all it reveals appear
pathetic in ignorance,
          like unconscious heroes trapped on film,
raised shadows about to descend and smash their skulls.

And when I'm not
unhappy but am
alone, then specially some hunger for revelation
keeps me up half the night
wandering from book to music to painting to book,
                              reluctant
to give any time at all to oblivion—

only the hope of memorable dreams
at last luring me
exhausted to bed.'

Now I can barely remember what it is
to want oblivion. 'The dreamy lamps
of stonyhearted Oxford Street'—
          de Quincy wandered
in hopeless search beneath them,

Olga rushed back and forth
for years beneath them, working
in her way for Revolution
and I too in my youth
knew them and was lonely, an ignorant girl.
But I forget anguish
as I forget joy

returning after 20 years
to 'merry London' as to a nest.

(Say what one will,
know what one must
of Powell, of the farm hand's
£13 a week—and they vote
Tory—yet

there is a gentleness
lost in anxious Amerika—

it's in the way
three young workmen in the Tube
smiled to each other
admiring their day-off purchases,
new shirts—

it's in the play-talk
of children, without irony:
not *cool,* not
joshing each other,

and in the way
men and women of any age maintain
some expectation of love,

(not pickups, but love) and so
remain beautiful:

there
      'in merry London, my most kindly nurse,
    that to me gave this life's first native source'

my friends whose lives
    have been knit with mine a quarter century
are not impaled on the spears of the cult of youth).
Aie, violent Amerika, aie, dynamic
deathly-sick America, of whose energy,
in whose fever, in whose wild
cacophonous music I have lived
and will live,

    what gentleness, what kindness
of the *private life* I left, unknowing,

and gained instead the tragic, fearful
knowledge of *present history,*
of doom. . . 'Imagination of disaster. . .life
ferocious and sinister'. . .

·

    But shall I forget
euphoria on the bus from
Trafalgar Square to Kings Cross?
      What a laugh,
there's nothing so great about Kings Cross,

but life is in me, a love for
what happens, for
the surfaces that are their own
interior life, yes, the
Zen buildings! the
passing of the
never-to-be-seen-again
faces! I bless

66

every stone I see, the
'happy genius' not of my household perhaps

but of my solitude. . .

vii

Two hours after reaching Rijeka
(that once was Fiume)
I'm drinking *vinjak* with five Sudanese.

(Four days ago I was in Dorset. We drank
cider and walked in the rain.)

Jugoslavia still unknown, mysterious,
slow train-ride, rocky fields in heat haze
                             and now
a roomful of subtle
black faces!
They refill my glass and give me
The Baghdad Observer: 'Al-Ali Reviews
Revolutionary Achievements.' I give them
the news about Bobby Seale.

I ask one for a towel,
he gives me his own.

I help clear the ash trays,
they say, No, that's *our* work.

They sing, and drum on whatever comes to hand,
(one makes a bell of knife and glass)
and two of them dance.
                             Outside,

oleanders astir in folds of
dense night.

To Abubakar I gave
my Panther button, the yellow one
with the great Black Cat emerging
in power from behind bars.

they read, and repeated it
to each other in Arabic.

And he gave me
a photo of turbanned dancers
and one of a bridge crossing the Blue Nile.

Abubakar, gat-toothed
like me.   'They say it's lucky,'
I told him, 'and means you will journey
very far.'

        In that room I knew the truth of what José
Yglesias writes, in his book on revolutionary Cuba that I'm
reading here on this Adriatic island 3 days later: he had
been to a film, a good one but these Cuban country people
took it with 'none of the tension, the concentration there
would have been in New York. . . . Their presence made me
see that for all its artistry . . . it was a false picture of life:
[they] knew that the easy-going goodness of people was
missing from it, that it allowed no avenue for joy, such as
they knew exists as soon as any bar to its enjoyment is let
down. Nor does it take a revolution to know this, just a bit
of living.'

And I remembered the time, just a few months ago,
a bitter March night in Boston, I went to see *Rock Around
the Clock* with Richard and Boat and someone else from
their collective, that was the same, gave me the same joy as
this roomful of friends, there was the same sense of generosity
and good humor, but more frantic, a sense of stolen time, of
pleasure only taken in recognition of desperate need *sometimes* to let up, a respite from the chills of fevered Amerika—

                    and here a leisure,
                    a courtesy unhurried
          as if the bare student pad
          were full of flowers, jasmine,
          roses . . .
                    Selah.
Abubakar—I gave him
my promise to find out in what country
he might enter medical school:
          'If I have to, I'll go
          to a capitalist country.'
And he (20, slender, beardless,
gentle, and warm to touch as a nectarine
ripe in the sun)

asked for and gave
a kind of love.

viii

After the American lava
has cooled and set in new forms,
will you Americans have
                    more peace and less hope?
wonders Sasha, socialist,
                    ('but not a Party member')

69

(We have not been asked, adds his wife

primly, the smallest smile
whisking across her elegant, honest face).

Is that what *you* have—
peace without hope?
                    I counter;

(and it seems perhaps
that *is* what they have
—at least,
none of the fervor here
that blazes in Cuban cane fields).

I swim out
over sharp rocks, sea urchins,
thinking, When I go back,

when I go back into the writhing lava,
will I rejoice in
fierce hope, in
wanhope, in
'righteous' pleasurable hope?

            Could struggle be enough, even
            without hope?

                        For that I'm not
                        enough a puritan. Or not yet.
                        (Richard might say: history intervenes
                        to weld endurance, revolution
            builds character—
                        but he is young,
            a young dreamer, wilful, stern).
                                    And peace—
I think I have
            not *hope* for it,
only a longing . . .

But on a hill in Dorset
    while the bells of Netherbury
    pealed beyond the grove of
    great beeches,
            and Herefords,
    white starred on tawny ample brows,
    grazed, slow, below us,
                only days ago,
Bet said:
There was a dream I dreamed always
over and over,

a tunnel
and I in it, distraught

and great dogs blocking
each end of it

and I thought I must
always go on
dreaming that dream,
trapped there,

but Mrs. Simon listened
and said

why don't you sit down
in the middle of the tunnel
quietly:

imagine yourself
quiet and intent sitting there,
not running from blocked
exit to blocked exit.

Make a place for yourself
in the darkness
and wait there. *Be* there.

The dogs
will not go away.
They must be transformed.

Dream it that way.
Imagine.

Your being, a fiery stillness,
is needed to TRANSFORM
the dogs.

And Bet said to me:
Get down into your well,

it's your well

go deep into it

into your own depth as into a poem.

'Let Us Sing Unto the Lord a New Song'

There's a pulse in Richard
that day and night says
revolution   revolution   revolution

and another
not always heard:

poetry   poetry

rippling through his sleep,
a river pulse.

Heart's fire
breaks the chest almost,
flame-pulse,
revolution:

and if its beat
falter
life itself
shall cease.

Heart's river,
living water,
poetry:

and if that pulse
grow faint
fever shall parch the soul, breath
choke upon ashes.

But when their rhythms
mesh
then though the pain of living
never lets up

the singing begins.

i   Report

I went back.
Daily life
is not lava.
            It is
a substance that expands and contracts, a rhythm
different from the rhythm of history,
though history is made of the same
minutes and hours.
                        Tony writes from Ohio:
                'An atomistic bleakness drags on students this fall
                after the fiery fusion of last spring.'

Airplane life: the fall for me
spent like a wildgoose that has lost
the migrating flock and lost
the sense of where the south is—
zigzagging—'gliding among clouds.'

England, back there in summer, and especially
the two Davids, turned out to be home: but my literal
home, these rooms, this desk, these small
objects of dailiness each with its history,
books, photos, and in the kitchen
the old breadknife from Ilford that says
Bread Knife on its blade—the least details—
are what pull me. No, it's not true that I'm
a defective migrant, I know as I fly
where I long to be. But the wind blows me
off course.

(Bromige writes: 'I recall the muffin man
too, and the naphtha lamps, I think they were, in the open-
air market, High Rd. Kilburn, after early December dark.
Now I sit up here on a California hillside. This difficulty of
what resonance has the language, for you, for me,—I need
to take up but the push and shove of events (that's a telling
phrase of Merleau-Ponty's!) has me, and meanwhile I go on
writing poems sometimes like shouting down a deep well.'

   Those are the same lamps
    of my dream of Olga—the eel or cockle stand,
    she in the flare caught, a moment, her face
    painted, clownishly, whorishly. Suffering.

'It's your own well.
Go down
into its depth.'

ii **Happiness**

Two nights dancing (Workingmen's Dead)
with someone of such grace and goodness, happiness
made real in his true smile,
       that it has seemed
I know now forever:
      The reason for happiness is,
      happiness exists.
Good Day Sunshine. The moon's vast aureole
of topaz was complete;
      utterly still;
        a covenant,
its terms unknown. / Waving arms! Swaying!
       The whirling of the dance!

Soon after
more (but not deeper) depth of joy
was given me at the show of Zen paintings.
                         Camus wrote:
       'I discovered inside myself, even in the very midst of
       winter, an invincible summer.'
Again—
           as in the act of clearing garbage off the land
together with those I loved,
and later dodging with them
                              the swinging clubs of the cops,
living
in that momentary community—
again happiness
astonished me, so easy, 'amazing grace.'
Easy as the undreamed
dreamlike reality
of Abubakar and his friends.

But before this
came the death of Judy. Yes,
Judy had killed herself a full two weeks
before my hours of dancing began,
I found out the night I read to raise money
for the Juche Revolutionary Bookstore,

iii   Two from the Fall Death-News

and still I've not begun the poem,
the one she asked for ('If you would write me a poem
I could live for ever'—postmarked
the night she died, October twenty-ninth.)
I've begun though
to gather up fragments of it,
fragments of her: the heavy tarnished
pendant I don't wear,

the trapped dandelion seed in its transparent cube,
three notched green stones for divination, kept
                                    in green velvet,
a set of the *Daily Californian* for all the days
of the struggle for the People's Park,
a thick folder of her letters,
and now (come with the Christmas mail, packed
in a pink cosmetic box grotesquely labelled,
        'The Hope Chest'),
four cassettes recording (or so they are marked,
I've not played them) her voice speaking to me . . .

Revolution or death. She chose
as her life had long foretold. I can't lose her,
for I don't love her. In all her carefully kept
but unreread letters, all I remember sharply is the green
cold of the water in the deep pool she evoked,
the rock pool said to be bottomless,
where as a young girl she swam naked, diving
over and over, seeking
to plumb its roaring silence.

                    • • • • • • • •

                    But Grandin, he could have lived!
His death, a year ago, hits me now,
reading his poems, stitched into order before he too
stopped himself.
                    Rage and awe
shake me.
And the longing to have spoken
long hours with him, to have gone
long walks with him beside rivers—
all I don't feel
for Judy, who in some fashion loved me,
lived through (for an hour, for recurring instants)
towards Grandin, to whom when he was alive
I was peripheral, as he to me . . .

78

'By the post house · windblown reed-fronds.
In some city tavern you dance the *Wild Mulberry Branch*.'
Rollicking, eyes flashing.   I resent your death
as if it were accidental.
          'Now snowstorms will fill the lands west of the Huai.
      I remember last year · broken candlelight upon
                              travelling-clothes.'
Last I heard of you, you were 'feeling better,'
up in some ghost town out West . . .
                                  I feel life in your words,
tortured, savage.
                    Further away than 17th-century China,
nearer than my hand, you smashed
the world in the image of yourself, smashed
the horror of a world lonely Judy,
          silently plunging forever
into her own eyes' icy green, never even saw;
you raged bursting with life into death.

iv   **Daily Life**

Dry mouth,
            dry nostrils.
Dry sobs, beginning
abruptly, continuing
briefly,
          ending.
                The heart
dragging back sand through steelblue veins,
scraping it back out into the arteries: and they take it.
Living in the gray desert and
getting used to it.   Years ago, Juan wrote:
'We can never forget ourselves, and our problems involve
others and deform them.'
                    And Hopkins:
            'Sorrow's springs are the same.'

79

Then rainbow day comes in flashing
off the snow-roofs. By afternoon, slogging
through falling snow,
yellow snowlight, traffic slowed to
carthorse pace,
    exhilaration, East Boston
doubling for London.
     I'm frivolous.
      I'm alone.
       I'm Miriam
(in *Pilgrimage*) fierce with joy
     in a furnished room near Euston.
I'm the Tailor of Gloucester's cat.
     I live in one day
a manic-depressive's year.
     I like
      my boots, I like
the warmth of my new long coat. Last winter
running through Cambridge with Boat and Richard, afraid of
       the ice they
slid on fearlessly—I must have been cold all winter
without knowing it, in my short light coat.
Buffalo Meat Market offers me a drink, (Strega),
     I lug home
the ham for Christmas Eve, life
whirls its diamond sparklers before me.
Yes, I want
   revolution, not death: but I don't
care about survival, I refuse
to be provident, to learn automechanics,
    karate,
    soybean cookery,
    or how to shoot.
  O gray desert,
  I inhabit your mirages,
  palace after palace. . .
    pineforest. . .
    palmgrove. . .

80

Judy ignored the world outside herself,
Grandin was flooded by it.
There is no suicide in our time
unrelated to history, to whether
each before death had listened to the living, heard
the cry, 'Dare to struggle,
            dare to win.'
heard and not listened, listened and turned away.

And I? 'Will struggle without hope
        be enough?' I was asking
on a sunny island in summer.
                            Now in midwinter
not doing much to struggle, or striving mainly
to get down into my well in hope
that force may gather in me
            from being still in the grim
            middle of the tunnel . . .
(And meanwhile Richard and Neil in their collectives
get down to it: get into work: food co-ops, rent strikes;
and 'Jacob and Lily' create
an active freedom in 'open hiding';
and Mitch has finished his book, 'a tool
for the long revolution.')
                        (And meanwhile Robert
                    sees me as Kali! No,
        I am not Kali, I can't sustain for a day
that anger.
            'There comes
                    a time
                    when only anger
                                is love'—
I wrote it, but know such love
only in flashes.

81

And the love that streams
towards me daily, letters and poems, husband and child,
sings . . .)

                  Mayakovsky wrote,
                  in the 3-stepped lines that Williams
                  must have seen and learned from,
'Life
      must be
            started quite anew,
when you've changed it,
               then
                    the singing can start up'—
but he too
took his own life. Perhaps he was waiting,
not with that waiting that is itself a
                        transforming energy—
          'Stone
          breaks stone to reveal
          STONE in stone!'—but waiting
to *set all things right,* (to 'rearrange all mysteries
                    in a new light')
before beginning to live? Not understanding
only conjunctions
            of song's
                raging magic
                with patient courage
                will make   a new life:
we can't wait: time is
              not on our side:
                    world
in which those I respect
                'already live, they're not waiting
for demolition and reconstruction.' No more
'learning as preparation for life.'
                    In my own days and nights
(crawling, it feels like, on hands and knees—leaping
up into the dance!—to fall again, sprawled, stupid—)

I'm trying to learn
the other kind of waiting: charge, or recharge, my
                                    batteries.
Get my head together. Mesh. Knit
idiom with idiom in the
'push and shove of events.'
                What I hold fast to
                is what I wrote last May, not Kali speaking:
            'When the pulse rhythms
            of revolution and poetry
            mesh,

            then the singing begins.'
                    But that *when* must be
                    now!
Timid, impatient, halfblinded by
the dazzling abyss, nauseous under
the roar of the avalanche,
'imagination of disaster' a poison
that lurches through me the way
a sickened killer might lurch
through streets of charred straw—
                        —what I hold fast to, grip
in my fist for amulet, is my love
of those who dare, who do dare
to struggle, dare to reject
unlived life, disdain
to die of *that*.
                'Let us become men' says Dan Berrigan.
                'Maybe you see it all, whiteman,
                        or maybe you blind,'
                    says Etheridge Knight to Dan.
                'We gotta work
                at our own pace, slow if need be,
                work together and learn from within,'
                    Richard said to me just today, the day
news of invasion of Laos started to be 'official.'

83

O holy innocents! I have
no virtue but to praise
you who believe
life is possible . . .

Some people mentioned in these poems. Dennis Riordon, Chuck Matthei, Bob Gilliam, David Worstell, de Courcy Squire and Jennie Orvino are young active war-resisters. Robert is the poet Robert Duncan, Bromige the poet David Bromige. Mitch is my husband Mitch Goodman; the trial referred to in 'Prologue: An Interim' is the one in which he, Dr. Benjamin Spock and three others were defendants. Richard, Boat and Neil are young members of revolutionary collectives. Other personal names refer to various friends, living and dead.

PAGE

10 The quoted lines—'a clearing/in the selva oscura, . . .'—are an adaptation of some lines in 'Selva Oscura' by the late Louis MacNeice, a poem muched loved by my sister, Olga.

29 *Life that/wants to live.* Albert Schweitzer's phrase, in formulating the basis of his sense of 'reverence for life': 'I am Life that wants to live, among other forms of life that want to live.'

29 *(Unlived life/of which one can die.)* Rilke's phrase from *The Notebook of Malte Laurids Brigge.*

33 Goldengrove/is unleaving all around me—refers to Gerard Manley Hopkins's 'Spring and Fall: To a Young Child.'

44 *Thursday, May 15th*—the day in 1969 when James Rector was killed, Alan Blanchard, an artist, blinded, and many people wounded by police buckshot fire while protesting the destruction of the People's Park.

46 WHAT PEOPLE CAN DO—from an issue of *The Instant News,* a daily information sheet published in Berkeley during the weeks of demonstrations.

51 *'Keiner/oder Alle, Alles/oder Nichts!'* The lines from Brecht are a refrain of a song about slaves casting off their chains: 'No one or everyone, all or nothing!'

56 'Casa Felice'—the house of friends on Cape Cod.

58 'I Thirst'—Words of Jesus from the Cross, according to John 19:28. The demonstration of May 9, 1970, attempted to make clear the relationship between war abroad and racism and political oppression at home.

65 Powell—the British right-wing politician Enoch Powell.

65 Tube—the London subway system.

66 'Imagination of disaster . . . life/ferocious and sinister'—Henry James, in a letter to Henry Adams.

85

68 José Yglesias—the quotation is from *In the Fist of the Revolution* (Vintage Books, New York, 1969, p. 89).

79 'By the post house . . . *Wild Mulberry Branch.*' 'Now snowstorms . . . travelling-clothes.' From a translation by David Lattimore of Mao Chi'i-ling, 'To the Air: Southern Branch (At an inn west of the Huai I receive a letter from Ch'en Ching-chih. Sent with a reply.)' See the *Brown University Alumni Monthly*, December, 1969.

81 Kali—the Hindu goddess of rage; the Black Mother.

82 Mayakovsky—the Russian poet Vladimir Mayakovsky (1893–1930). The quotation is from his *How Are Verses Made?* (G. M. Hyde, tr., Grossman, 1970). Though William Carlos Williams did not read Russian, he did *see* Mayakovsky's poems; and though his own structural inventions came out of rhythmic, sonic, expressive necessities of his own, I surmise the visual impression of Mayakovsky's lines may have remained with him as a hint. See his 'Russia,' first published in *The Clouds* (1948), and included in *The Collected Later Poems* (New Directions, 1963).

82 'Stone/breaks stone. . . .' From an inscription on an ancient Chinese painting, 'Hamlet Between Cliffs,' by Tao Chi.

83 'Let us become men'—adapted from what Father Berrigan said in his last 'underground' speech, before his recapture in 1970, at a rally in support of the people who had destroyed draft files by immersing them in chemicals manufactured by the Du Pont Corporation. He said, in part: 'Let us therefore trust what we have done. Let us multiply the same and similar acts. Let us trust one another. Let us draw near across great differences, exorcize together our fear. Let us do that one thing . . . which by common and cowardly agreement is forbidden in America today—let us be men.'

83 Etheridge Knight—the poet, editor and part author of *Black Voices from Prison*. The quotation is from 'To Dan Berrigan,' in the November, 1970, issue of *Motive,* of which Knight is poetry editor; the magazine also carried the text of Father Berrigan's speech, cited above.